© 2022 Experiments in Fiction.

BARBARA HARRIS LEONHARD
THREE-PENNY MEMORIES: A POETIC MEMOIR

All rights reserved. No part of this publication may be reproduced, stored in a retrieval system or transmitted in any form or by any means, electronic, mechanical, photocopying, recording or otherwise without the prior permission of the publisher or the author of the relevant work who retains the copyright of his work in accordance with the provisions of the Copyright, Designs and Patents Act 1988 or under the terms of any license permitting limited copying issued by the Copyright Licensing Agency.

ISBN: 978-1-7397577-6-2

Barbara Harris Leonhard

Three-Penny Memories:
A Poetic Memoir

About the Author

Barbara Harris Leonhard's work appears in various online and print publications and anthologies. The most recent anthology, *Wounds I Healed: The Poetry of Strong Women* (Ed. Gabriela Marie Milton, 2022) was a #1 bestseller on Amazon. Barbara earned both third place and honorary mention for two poems in *Well Versed* 2021. *Three-Penny Memories: A Poetic Memoir* is her debut poetry collection.

The poem "Marie Kondo Cleans My Purse at Starbucks" was voted Spillwords Publication of the Month of January and February 2022. Barbara was also voted Spillwords Author of the Month of October 2021 and recognized as a Spillwords Socialite of the Year in 2021. Barbara enjoys hosting Zoom gatherings for poets. You can follow her on WordPress - Extraordinary Sunshine Weaver.

Barbara lives in Missouri with her husband Dierik, a musician of Bluegrass, Cajun, and Country music, and their cat Jasper. As well as writing poetry, she enjoys creating collages and neurographic art.

Praise for Three-Penny Memories: A Poetic Memoir

"Barbara Leonhard has given us a memoir that is an intricately woven tapestry of loss, grief, and struggle for reconciliation. She is an archeologist sifting for news of a maternal relationship buried in hurt and anxiety. Alzheimer grabbed her mother and she was dragged down into that shadowy abyss. What disappeared with her are the answers to the questions a desperate daughter mourns and carries through each day. When her mother moves in with her daughter, a shattering doubt enters through the door with her. Is the daughter's care given out of love or obligation? Is Three Penny Memories careless change or rare coins that glitter in a corner of the excavation of Leonhard's family? Only the reader can decide. A stunning first book!"

Walter Bargen, Missouri's first Poet Laureate, author of several books, including *My Other Mother's Red Mercedes*, *Pole Dancing in the Nightclub of God*, and *You Wounded Miracle*.

"Ever since Barbara Leonhard's first submission to Free Verse Revolution, her work has been a pleasure to read. Leonhard is a storyteller; her poetry shares lived experience as well as narratives she has listened to or witnessed in her writing journey. Her work is always refreshingly honest and human, In fact, I find her portrayal of a parent/child relationship in this collection to be incredibly raw and moving. And it has been particularly special to experience the development of Leonhard's craft over the past few years. I am grateful to have worked with Barbara Leonhard and to have published many of her poems about her and her mother. It is about time these pieces had a very special home of their own, in this collection."

Kristiana Reed, Editor-in-Chief, Free Verse Revolution: a literary magazine

"I really resonated with these very moving and haunting poems... marvelous work."

James Diaz, Poetry Editor, Anti-Heroin Chic

This collection includes "much to admire, including the depths explored in these poems of the mother-daughter relationship, how the past and present connect (and disconnect) through memory and memory loss, and the perceived sincerity of the speaker's voice."

Jill McCabe Johnson, Editor-in-Chief, Wandering Aengus Press and Trail to Table Press

THREE-PENNY MEMORIES

A Poetic Memoir

BARBARA HARRIS
LEONHARD

*How can a daughter question her love for her mother
while helping her to navigate the progression of Alzheimer's?
Can she learn to love the stranger
that her mother has become?*

DEDICATED TO MY MOTHER
BARBARA MONTGOMERY HARRIS
(02/28/1927 – 04/03/2016)

Where Thou art,
That is home.
-Emily Dickinson

Contents

Excavating the Heart Wall of Grief	19

LIGHT — 21

Mother's Light	23
Hyperion Raises Doubts	25
Hestia for Hire	28
Daughter, Like Mother	30
The Bear Went over the Mountain	32
My Memoir as a Doll	34
This Brittle Seed	38
I Love You So Much It Hurts	41
Mom's Little Mommy	43
Bearing the World	45
Picking Blueberries with Mom	46
Our House of Hungers	48
"Mrs. Sibley's Ghost is Passing Through."	53
My Mother's Vanity	57
It Builds Character	60
Cooking a Life with a Wire Spine	61
The Wounded	65
Mom's Song - and Dance	66
Mom's *DES Baby*: The Hardest Pill to Swallow	68
Ode to the Embryo that My T-Shaped Uterus Miscarried	70
Woman	72

2 DUST 73

Erosion	75
Winning the Lottery	76
Trip to Gehenna	78
Mom's Journal	82
Bundling Blankets	84
Mom's Pickles	86
Mom's Never Wrong	89
Held without Bond	93
Playing Cards Right	95
Holding Out Soap	97
Senior Alert	99
Irish Spring	102
The Caregiver's Craft	106
An Unsanctioned Outing	108
Mom's Purse	113
Bookends	115
Grandmother Lilian	118
Mom and I Play Lassos with Our Hysterectomy Scars	121
Mud Maid	124

3	ECHO	**125**

I Betray Her	127
House of Sand	129
Mom and Elvis	132
Fool's Gold	134
The Marauding Jackals	136
Angels Give a Hoot	138
Departing from Gate 3	142
Mermother: A Rogue Dream Poem	145
Mom's Dreams	147
The Phone of the Wind	150
Marie Kondo Cleans My Purse at Starbucks	153
Mom's Promise	156
Farewell, My Flower	157
"Thinking of You"	159
Acknowledgments	163

Excavating the Heart Wall of Grief

I excavate my soul. Salvage the shards
that comprise my mosaic. Brush away the shades
of a soiled past. Striking something hard,
I coax it loose. Examine it. Toss it aside.

Some fragments yield to my touch; others cut.
I must dredge the diamantine dark
to dismantle the heart wall of grief. Even if
there is bloodletting.

Mother's sorrow, inherited from her mother.
The law of abandoned excavations.
Some artifacts, buried so deep
the air there coughs up afflictions.

I'm the mandala passed down
from mother to daughter,
mother to daughter,
mother to daughter.

I have no daughters, no lineage.
My mother's unwitting mistake.
Bad medicine stole my womb. Can I
transmute the loss into a healing salve?

As I break down the walls, other stories
tumble out. My childhood illness
and a miscarriage. Our near deaths.
Broken wombs. Secrets aslant.

The arcs of two lives
stretch into a double rainbow.
A mother-daughter love story
the hue of copper. The expanse
        into light, dust, echo.

1

LIGHT

"Do You Love Your Mother?"

Mother's Light

I.
Mother's light guides me to her.
To her wound. I descend
into her balefire. Birth scraps

a scar on my neck.
I cleave to her, suckle loss.
As soon as I am born,

I start saying goodbye.
Nothing lasts. Except scars.
Love makes me her namesake,

her likeness in miniature,
her wound's creation. My parents'
elixir. They raise their grail.

II.
When a baby's born,
all mothers sigh in unison,
a butterfly effect,

rippling into all mothers' souls
then to the planets and stars,
searching for names.

My grandmothers and great-grandmothers
were generous with births.
Most had 6 or 7.

There were tragedies.
The two baby sisters Mom lost,
creating a hole in Grandmother Lilian's soul

that mother could not fill.
The wound of the mother
becomes the wound of the daughter.

My mother felt abandoned
by her mother, just as her mother
felt abandoned by her baby daughters.

Grief is a shared malady.
It drains the pond.
No amount of tears

can repair the hemorrhage.
Healing is not always glorious.
Though light guides and softens pain,

it can singe as a wild fire.
Creation of life and love
is as chaotic as star birth.

Hyperion Raises Doubts

I.
"You love her?" My uncle asks.
    "Excuse me, what?"

"Your mother, Hon. Do you love her?"
    OK. Wait now.

Why ask this? Why question my devotion?
    She's my mother!

"Course I do!" Still, I wonder,
    given he asks.

My favorite uncle - he should know!
    Now I'm curious -

maybe even confused. He raises incertitude.
    Have they talked?

Are there secrets? What have I done?
    Am I uncaring?

II.
She nearly dies from a very low pulse.
        How long did she suffer?

She needs a pacemaker. A loyal daughter,
        I rescue her.

This woman arrives. Rather odd.
        Sits alone, quiet.

Rebuffing me? Why so remote?
        What's the matter?

She's managed flights. The lay-overs,
        meals, her bags.

She isn't steady. Needs assistance.
        Why so helpless now?

Oh, Lord, the stairs! Peril is everywhere.
        Like bear traps.

III.
I can't sleep. Neither can she.
    It's four a.m.

She gets dressed. "What's up, Mom?"
    I guide her downstairs

where we wait. I ponder our love
    until the sun rises,

slowly revealing the face
    of someone's mother.

Hestia for Hire

I.
My last visit before Dad died. Tears, drained ponds.
There they sit. The loud TV. Their separate recliners.
Mom's endless romances. Never engaging me, except for meals.

I clean, cook. Do laundry, scrub. Daughter or maid?
Waiting for inquiries. "How's your life? Are you happy?"
Mother points down. "There's a spill." *Cabernet or blood?*

Many dead plants. "Use the disposal." *It's a tree!*
The disposal groans. Tree legs shred. Like grinding bones.
The fingers snap. Time to eat. Frozen dinners, salads.

One heart attack. Then two strokes. Dad's emaciated, slow.
He hauls oxygen. Mom awaits rescue. Dad throws kisses.
I do dishes. They don't notice. I slip away.

Walking, thinking, sobbing. Lake, geese, goslings.
The ganders honking.

II.
The phone rings. Their eyes roll. It's a sister.
Arriving for Christmas! Dad asks why. "I'll be gone."
He takes off before dawn's light in early December.

The family gathers. A Christmas funeral to celebrate Dad.
A small reunion, what Mom wants. She arrives first.
Without any luggage. Unkept, bedraggled, aloof.

She doesn't explain. We go shopping. Dresses, panties, nighties.
She sits alone, not facing us. These ominous signs.
We miss them – or deny them.

She worsens, alone. Never calls us. Her heart, slowly dying.
Then the call from her friend. "Come get her!"
The missing daughter. I feel rebuked. Forgotten duties, obligations.

A mother's decline. A daughter's agony.
       My fears, tears.
Love is gentle. Love is kind.
       Love can burn.

Daughter, Like Mother

"Do you love her?" Those haunting words.
        I seek counseling.

Grief awaits cure. List life traumas.
        Where to begin?

Grief emerges in the young. With birth, there is loss.
        Mom's swaddling womb, my evictor.

A shy child, I am clinging, tremulous.
        Have panic attacks in the first grade.

I am six going on seven. Measles encephalitis cripples.
        Paralysis, coma, and a near death.

Heaven says, "No." My second birth –
        into a wheelchair, isolation, loneliness.

Grief, heavy, burying brittle seed
        in Earth's womb. I'm trapped in the chair.

From Mom, the gumption to walk again
        when doctors said "No."

Brain damage aftermath of encephalitis. Tears, constant crying.
        Problems with learning.

I lack confidence, withdraw. Bullies torment me.
    Mom, my comforter.

I look back at this viral swelling plague.
Many memories, extinguished.

I can relate, Mom, to how histories crumble.
    How memories burn off
        like the dew in hot sun.

Our paths align. You held me;
    Now I hold you.

The Bear Went over the Mountain

I.
A month-long coma from encephalitis,
I awaken in a cold, searing light.
A man in white. *Am I dead?*

"The bear went over the mountain. Say it, dear."

"The bear went over the mountain."

"She'll be fine."

The needles pricking my legs
can't make them move. Mother always believes
a doctor's prognosis.

"But she won't walk again."

II.
I never consider Mom's ability
to be at my side daily yet still care
for three other children, one a baby.

The story books. Her gifts of ice cream cones.
One day, I trick her into giving up
both cones. I ask for the chocolate one,

her choice. Then delight in the licorice one,
eating both so fast that the ice cream
doesn't melt. Like my gratitude does.

III.
Mom, my She Bear. Her quick bite.
She growls. Chases off the strangers
who enter my room and loom

over my paralyzed body.
Claws at the impatient nurse
who leaves me on the toilet for two hours.

Mom never complains
about my level of care. Instead,
she holds me in my despair.

My Memoir as a Doll

I.
Memories, bubbles burst by encephalitis.
Neurons, drowned by viral swell.
I cling to these scenes. Minnesota.

A baby, touching snow for the first time.
A toddler, rocking in a chair.
My pet dog no one else can see.

Kindergarten, the little kitchen.
Pots, pans, dishes, an oven.
Bossing the boys. Our heckled husbands.

Kool-Aid and cookies.
Story time in a circle.
Nap time on braided rugs.

II.
The move to Montana.
Grandma Hattie's stroke.
Her room off the kitchen.

Mom, her caregiver.
Our finding Grandma
passed away on my first day of school.

My panic attack while entering
the First-Grade classroom that day.
The teacher's desk, looming up

like a grizzly. Its hot breath
burns my lungs, molten grief.
One day, Mom sends me upstairs.

Another errand. My legs
give out. My Mount Everest,
the stairs. I descend with a slide.

Call to Mom. Unable to walk,
to reach for hugs, to speak, to eat solids.
Mom feeds me baby food. I'm her doll to haul.

The couch, my new bed. Convenient.
Joyous sounds from the kitchen. People pass by
my dusty porcelain shell.

Loneliness. Helplessness. My sister
tries to visit. My words, clear in my mind,
befuddled squawks to her. I grow mute.

My parents rushing home one night.
My siblings' eyes frighten me.
The cold car. Mom's lap. The blackness.

III.
I get to see Grandad, who's in the same hospital.
I'm standing by his bed. We visit
and laugh. I want to go with him.

The people there say, "No."
I argue. They insist I return to my room.
I scold them with my eyes.

I don't know that these tall figures in white
are angels. My soul is spared
for Grandpa's by this holy council.

IV.
I awaken to the cold blast
of a burning heaven. White figures hover.
I repeat their prayers. They rejoice

about pulling the strings
and pose this Paralyzed Barbie
under a sheet.

V.
The return home in a wheelchair.
The people waiting for me. The party.
The gifts. A tea set I've always wanted.

They speak over me. I'm invisible.
Still carried, washed and dressed.
My parents' gratitude

and grief. My friends outside. I miss
the breeze and tease. The running.
Hide and Seek. Hot sunny days.

VI.
Late back to school. Second grade.
Diseased Barbie. Forced to sit in the hall.
Kids run past me quickly.

Slow Learner Barbie. Lack of focus.
Poor memory. Constant crying.
Effects of encephalitis.

Now I'm "other". Friendless.
An easy target for teasing. Cruel remarks.
For me, not this life. Not now.

Too young to suffer as Fragile Barbie. Too young
to be cast into an empty plastic shell,
posed in this wheelchair.

Where's my soul? My voice?
My strength? My will?
I call them back to their ghost.

This Brittle Seed
> *Reflections on Surviving Measles Encephalitis*

My body, a cage.
Only eyes for doors.
My arms, contorted branches,
twist in shadows.
Voices, hollow sounds,
call from the dinner table.
My legs, dead trunks,

hold me to the couch.
A view to other children,
dancing pansies and violets,
their blooms outstretch
to gather rays.
Each day a storm clashes in my core
to trigger genesis. Lightning misfires.

Mother's tunes carry me to the clouds.
My lips mute my longing.
Cries muffle in my throat.
Each wail, the language of stones,
falls on deaf ears.
I cannot move.

> *I'm still in here.*
> *Don't forget the light*
> *inside this frail seed*

*afflicted with blight.
I'm stuck in mud,
too dense for birth;*

*too turbid for food.
No gardener to churn the soil.
To feed me air.*

I am buried. New blooms
swaddled in violet and pink
dance on my grave. Beckon.
      "Come and play; the day is divine."
I claw my way
out of the stiff core,
muck and stone

into a blinding light.
My arms and fingers unfold
into new green.
My tiny legs stretch into roots
holding my core as it sways
in buoyant breeze
that warms my face.

A flower can't remain
as a seed forever.
It casts its casing aside
in a mighty battle to forge a life.
Even the brittle seed
can bloom. For this one,
        hope was not a loss.

I Love You So Much It Hurts

"Thereby hangs a tale," Dad writes,
announcing the birth
of his youngest, the seventh,
9 pounds 3 ounces,
at 2:45am on Mother's Day, 1961.

Five hours later,
Mom's hemorrhaging. Surgery
fails to stop the bleeding.
Blood transfusions, 20 pints,
into both arms

through cut-downs
at her wrists and elbows.
Later that day,
a total hysterectomy.
Four days after the 21st transfusion,

a near mortal reaction.
Partial collapse of her left lung.
Pneumonia.
Her incision opens.
An abscess develops

in her abdomen.
Nearly a three-week hospital stay,
24 pints of blood
in 26 administrations.
Vacation time for Dad to cook, clean,

tend to the baby.
A home nurse, 8 hours a day
for a long year
of immobility and healing.
The wound crusts over
        a mother's tenacious love.

Mom's Little Mommy

I.
Mom has three. One more five years later.
>Then births twins. Under hypnosis.

One year later. Her seventh emerges,
>a hefty boy. She almost dies at 34.

I'm just 10, the eldest daughter. My sister and I,
>little mommies and maids.

II.
Mom's laborious healing. She's the helpless observer.
>Our commotion, theatrics for her amusement.

So many diapers - cloth back then.
>The rinsing in buckets.

The washing, drying, folding. The pinning to babies.
>Sorry, some accidents.

Bottles to sterilize. Food to prepare.
>My sister and I queue up the babies.

One spoon in. One spoon out.
>I move on.

My sister follows. One bottle in.
    One bottle out.

III.
I wake my baby siblings
    to rock and to love them.

Then one day, his tiny lips part.
    The seventh says, "Muh. Muh."

Mother's face falls. The sound, "Mama",
    a bittersweet reminder and foreboding.

I run outside to water my flowers.
    The soil, dry, undernourished.

My violets, dry of tears. Mom's birth-month flower.
    My black thumb.

Bearing the World

Your equator is full.
I hold your globe and press my ear
against your skin to hear

the heartbeat of another new sun,
its glow flickering,
a mysterious creation

held in warm waters.
Soft waves lap to the tiny heartbeat.
Your water breaks and floods the home

with babies, diapers, pacifiers, toys.
I learn to swim to rescue you
from drowning

and think someday I too will
bear the world
and pack my chest of hopes

with bibs, blankies, bottles.
My dreams leave no sound as they settle
into shadows.

My ghosts, swaddled
in umbra.

Picking Blueberries with Mom

The hot summer Michigan days.
Mom loves picking wild blueberries.
That promised family vacation
to the beach of Lake Michigan.
Cut short at the sight

of patches of wild blueberries
in a meadow drenched in searing sun.
We barrel out of the car
on the dusty road for her sake
to scatter in the patches. - Frankly,

berry picking. Not my love.
We're heading one place
only to be sidetracked.
Our trip to the lake, postponed.
Mom takes to the field

like a young girl,
her smock, stained blue. Her lips
made ready for purple kisses.
I keep watch on the tree lines
for hungry bears.

She's lost in the foraging.
Requires us to gather
what we can in our shirts.
My back aches as I do this work.
I impatiently wait

to be on our way. To seek relief
in cool lake water. Away from bees,
mosquitoes and biting flies.
Mom sings as she picks. Her tunes
resound as prayers. Blueberries

bring forth blessings. Eternal optimism.
Mom's radiant, recapturing the time
her mother took her to her first blueberry patch,
where she learned to halt time
and sing in meadows.

Our House of Hungers

I.
Dad, his own best friend.
Adventures on the sandy beach
of Lake Michigan, his playground

for swimming and skating.
Nature musters legends.
The winter snow eats him,

buries him up to the neck.
Another boy, wearing Dad's skates,
falls through the lake ice.

II.
Our arrivals to his family lake house
to surprise our grandparents.
Our faces burn

in Grandpa's whisker kisses. Grandma Hattie,
always in a cotton flowered apron.
Always in the kitchen.

Our tummies, filled with her cherry pie.
The gaiety at the round kid table
by the wood-burning stove. The hours of play

on the beach. Our fun blazes into blisters.
Bandages, our body armor.
Grandma's hugs burst our suns.

III.
Years pass away. Our grandparents
smile in frames. Our move back
to Dad's family home as he departs

for a year at Princeton
for a Master's in Theology.
Alone with seven kids,

Mom resolves to survive
this sacrifice. The house eats
her burdens. Our messy litter

of candy wrappings, toys,
mountains of laundry. Her heirloom jewelry
feeds the vents.

A bag of flour spreads a fine rug
for visitors due any minute.
The lid on an open tuna fish can

almost severs my little brother's toes
as he vaults from the dining room table
on a dare. Blood. Mayhem. The ER.

Once the house almost dies
in a violent lightning storm.
While Mom is across the street,

a fiery bolt sears the side of the house
next to my big brother's head.
Hit by the flu, all of us pale,

wretch. Even the house
spews laundry down the stairs.
Stinks of sour milk. Unwashed diapers.

IV.
In winter the hungry house
waits for coal delivery.
When fed, the house shakes

like a beast, choking out smoke
and dust. In front of the open mouth
of the furnace,

a woman stabs the coals.
Her eyes blaze
as though scathed to the fire.

"Mom?" I whisper.
Her head snaps around.
"What!!"

I flee to my bedroom,
where the window opens
a portal onto the frozen lake.

Moonlight splinters
into twisted shadows on the shore.
My screams scrape a dance on the ice.

As the night air echoes
the howls of wolves,
the ice gives way.

V.
The musty smell
of Granddad's rusty tools
in the garage.

The kitchen steams memories
of Grandma Hattie's fresh-baked bread
and hot cocoa.

I search for Mother's lost pearls.
Scrub the floors of coal dust.
Collect driftwood for the mantel.

Mom emerges from the house.
"This way", she says. "We can't
linger here."

I fear the water.
Dare not venture too far.
She beckons,

"Follow. Follow."
We sink to the deep lake bottom
of drowned brush.

Twist with the current.
Eat the sweet and sour remains
of recollections.

"Mrs. Sibley's Ghost is Passing Through."[1]

"Relax, unbend. Have a good time."[2]
The motto in your 1945-46 Lindenwood
College Freshman Handbook

for picnics and parties in October.
The Halloween Queen,
crowned at the Masquerade Party,

wore chiffon. What was your costume, Mom?
The ghost of Mrs. Sibley,
her haunting organ tunes at midnight

in Sibley Chapel. Did you see her
pass through the halls? Did she keep a keen eye
on you girls? Make sure that you smiled?

In December, did you help dress dolls
for the children at Markham Settlement House?
(You always knitted, crocheted and sewed for us.)

In January, did you return from break
with pictures of a handsome beau,
as the college handbook promised?

---

1   Lindenwood College, "Lindenwood Handbook: 1945-1946", 15.
2   Ibid.

Did you entertain soldiers and sailors
at the "home front" to help the war effort?
To build morale? Did you stroll

with a man in uniform under the stars
at the St Louis Arch or along the river's edge -
or did you study for finals?

Was that when you left? You didn't
finish the year. Was it difficult being
almost 800 miles away from home?

Was it stressful to be the perfect lady?
It shows in your yearbook photograph.
All the young freshman women,

wearing the same starched smile. Groomed
to dress well. To serve – especially
to reconstruct society after the war.

You learned how to be casual,
but not careless. The appropriate garments
for classes, campus events, dinner, dates,

dances, formal teas, walks in the woods,
picnics, and trips into St Louis.
This prestigious women's college

first managed by the Presbytery of St. Louis –
Your family, Presbyterians. The ideal school
for an innocent woman. Values

and traditions. Structure and safety.
Just as Mary Easton Sibley expected
in her boarding school that grew

into Lindenwood College. To hone young women
in matters of courtesy, punctuality,
elegance, citizenship, sociability,

excellence in studies, duty.
Mom, did you keep your room in order?
Greet faculty with formality?

Have perfect attendance
at the daily assemblies, convocations,
and vespers? Above all, did you smile?

Without fail? Smile?
Did you graciously sacrifice
the regular dinner menu

for the many "Bean Soup Suppers"
to help the college save money
for the war effort?

BARBARA HARRIS LEONHARD

What did the ghost of Mrs. Sibley say
when you felt the need to walk away
into a new day?

My Mother's Vanity

Mom's cedar beauty station,
        where I primp.
My desire to see *her* face.
        Her shimmer of hair.
The light splashing
        on *her* Bésame lips.

I dabble in dreams.
        Twist my hair and clamp it
in coils with her bobby pins.
        Fluff the curls to my shoulders
for a night out.

My face will light up at a stop
        to view the moon. I'll feel
the cool, surrounding darkness
        undrape my skin.

The long mirror swings on hinges.
        Faces their bed. The sun whispers
off the bed linens. I gingerly open
        the vanity drawer.

    Follow a thread of pearls
winding deep into Mom's memories.
        Past Grandmother Lilian's rings.
A bottle of red polish.
        Black and white Kodak photos

of Mom at my age. A girl fumbling
        for freedom. Cooing for caresses.
Another of her as a college coed.
        Her head turns to the call of her name.

The light from her eyes slips
        into a coy smile. Her lips part
into a hush. Waves of desire
        crease folds into a sublime form.
A pearl earring reflects a new dream.

Shadows entwined on soiled sheets.
        Mistakes made, shame.
              Her father's scorn.
Her mother's cold silence.

My hands retreat,
    bitten by the snake.

        I excavate more memories,
    kicked under floorboards,
        polished to cover gouges
in the wood panels.

        Stomped on. Scuffed by flights
from hall mirrors.
        Not for my eyes
            to see
                what remains.

        Red nail clippings.
Stained hankies.
        Broken clasps. An unthreaded
            strand of pearls.

It Builds Character

Hold in your tummy
when you walk, or else,
you won't be pretty. I want you girls

to do the dishes for Mrs. Smith
after dinner with them on Saturday.
By the way, everyone can see you passing notes

in the choir. Stop twisting your hair
when you talk to those boys
across the street. It will only

make trouble.
Sit with your knees together.
Feet on the floor.

Return to the store this minute and tell them
they gave you too much change.
We want you home by 9:00

unless you finish your chores.
Then 9:30. But if you stay home
from school or church,

don't expect to go anywhere.
Stop crossing your eyes.
They'll freeze in place.

Cooking a Life with a Wire Spine

The recipe book that Mom assembled
in her own hand.
The front cover, missing.
The coffee-stained pages,
some partly dislodged
from the braided wire spine. Recipes

harvested from lineages
stuck together by spilled batter.
Mistakes. Lessons learned. The hard way.
Trial and error. Until you got it right.
Without burning your hands.
Without blood splatter.

Mom, a complex feast of sour and sweet,
had her edge. Bitter, black coffee.
If provoked, she whistled steam
and blew her top. Like when I started
shaving my legs. Dared to wear her lipstick.
Even worse, eye shadow and mascara. Worse yet,

miniskirts and halter tops.
I took her as she was.
Neither gluten free nor fat free.
Nor sugar free. She was pie crust made with lard.
Beef roast trimmed with fat.
The crisp skin on the holiday bird.

The full plate. No waste.
You didn't hide the scrambled eggs
behind the radio.
      "You eat it all.
      Or you don't eat.
      Finish your plate!"

She served us portions Dad could eat.
      "A sin to have skinny kids!"
She made sure I carried my weight,
knowing the dimples of gluten
under the skin would repel love
and dissuade any dream to be a cheerleader.

Mom's soft side. Hot cinnamon rolls.
Fried donuts, spun in sugar.
Pillowy loaves of white bread
hot from the oven, smothered
in sticky strawberry kisses.
She transformed want into wonder,

magically feeding seven insatiable kids
on a budget of $100 a month. Turning
our whines into hot bouillon.
Stretching homemade pizza
onto twelve cookie sheets. Mom's back,
tempered cast iron.

A spiral wire holding it all together -
These recipes of holy perfection.
    "When you cook,
        you go by the book."
I proceeded only with a nod of her head.
Learned not to overmix the muffins.

Or bake in a naked pan.
Or cut into the sacred loaf
before it's ready.
    "No one wants a mismeasured life.
    A cake that falls. Crumbs in your frosting.
    Taste as you go. Don't just dump it all in.

    Too much pepper chokes the throat."
Like Virginia Slims do,
so I dared not smoke –
or – God Forbid - do pot.
She would know and rise up
like yeasty dough

on a steamy summer day
to shuck and can me.
I watch creamer swirl in my cup
and wipe another spill
from a page of the recipe book
with the wire spine

that binds me to her
and wonder when - if ever –
I can begin to date
or learn to drive and get my own car
without her coming
        to a full boil.

The Wounded

Mom, your soldiers fought in World War II;
mine in Vietnam. Mrs. Sibley's ghost approved
your entertaining homesick sailors and soldiers
at the Gateway to the West –
provided you wore the proper apparel.

I wave at the sailors at the Soo Locks
and dance with lonely Kincheloe airmen
at a smoky bar at the wharf. Mrs. Sibley disapproves
of my halter top and bell bottoms. Sees to it
the ghost from Old Fort Brady

guards my walks home, where you wait
at the window off the porch. You know the scent
of the wounded on my breath.
One day, I dare say, "birth control".
You scream like an air raid siren. Dad

covers the windows. Locks the doors.
Your home, my anchor hold. The shadows
of the wounded pass by the porch window
for poems and blessings. But you forbid me to speak
their language of loneliness.

Mom's Song - and Dance

Do linden leaves cry as they release
their grasp from their Mother's skirt?
How does she feel when her bounty
loses grip? Her children, her color burst.
Their song to her in crisp wind play.
Their poetry, how it beds their paths.
As more let go, they reveal the clouds,
gray with drifts of snow that blanket
Mother's heart until the day she dons
her spring attire for Easter prayer. That is -

    until her oldest girls, both adults,
        announce their departure
  to their own place, a small apartment
        next to the church!

  My sister and I conspire,
        after counseling with Apate,
  to cut the roots, transplant
        ourselves. Thrive in new soil.

  Apate has prepared us for their terror,
        their agonizing throes, their many deaths.
  Mother threatens another heart attack
        for Dad, who threatens to stab himself.

The down payment made,
    the lease signed. No turning back.
I am anxious, having failed my parents.
    Indeed, while shopping,

she stops strangers to tattle, "My daughters,
    up and leaving. So ungrateful.
After all I've done. They're
    the death of me. And their father!"

My sister and I settle in.
    Remaster our lives.
Mother still bakes pies,
    sharpens knives.

Mom's *DES Baby*: The Hardest Pill to Swallow

I dig into the edge of grief. Unhealed betrayal.
Childless because of Mom, who never doubts
a doctor's word. She's spotting, fears losing me.
Is prescribed Diethylstilbestrol (DES). Blesses me

with a T-shaped uterus, infertility, cancer threats.
Tumors abound. Breasts, thyroid, uterus.
A pregnancy, possible, but not viable.
My deformed uterus delivers pain.

How can I cuddle
this bloody mass?

Mom is beset. To reassure her, I lose my need
for her hugs. Hold her grief in my broken womb.
Her comfort first. Does she see me? I sting of shame,
dismissed. How she forgets!

One day says – out of nowhere –
shattering words out of her scattered mind,
"You're still childless? Don't know why!
I dropped seven!"

I dig deeper. Uproot the past. Undergo major extractions.
Swallow the dirt - A total hysterectomy.
A partial thyroidectomy. All tumors benign.
Cancers caught in time.

Still, I grieve. My womanhood, aborted.
My eggs, dispatched as biohazard.
My hollow earth. My barren feminine.
My broken lineage.

Now I'm "other", watching young mothers.
How they procreate. Carry their worlds.
The ecstatic births. The breastfeeding.
All the sacrifices. All the stories.

Never a mother except to my own.
I'm her cane, her calendar, her brain.
My uncle asks, "Do you love your mother?"
My soul asks, "Have you healed the wound?"

Unearthing my trauma,
I swaddle my aging mother
to birth myself.

Ode to the Embryo that My T-Shaped Uterus Miscarried

You left my broken womb
as the bloody remains of what
was never to come. I still feel you
in the waves, the flow
of my sacral river - your tears?

Your fears I've abandoned you?
No, Honey. No! I'll never forget you.
The t-shaped womb
couldn't hold your brilliance.
Your tiny, beautiful self,

washed away. Your light
sparkles in each of my cells.
My core, your forever home.
Your essence, my creative labor
in verse and art.

Everyone says, "Forget the dead."
I can't leave my baby
screaming in her forever crib.
Or my young miss alone
in harm's way on grief's edge.

Though never delivered
into my arms, you shelter
in my wound of wanting. Each night,
I press my scar against a pillow
to swaddle you in your mother's heat.

In dreams, we share the sacred skiff,
and together, wind up and up
out of the wake
of the wound
into a newborn sky.

Woman

For Mom

    Woman, how you portray
    your complex essence and ambiguity.

You are a study of light
cast on the walls of your Self.

    Shadows border your brilliance.

Your portrait is askew with flavors
that you offer to guests

    enamored by your mystery
    as you gaze into obscurity.

2

DUST

"Mom, you can't live with me."

Erosion

A garden once planted in spring,
bearing life in shade and sun,
now tangled with weeds and blight.

A hearty yield once sustained
by dew and noon rains,
now forgets in autumn light.

Basket of Gold, having bloomed
and stretched for sun,
now shrivel, scorched by drought.

Honeysuckle, a trespasser in flora,
once nurtured monarchs
and bees.

Once a bounty of bliss,
now wild bramble
on depleted soil.

Wisdom of soils and seedlings,
now crumbles to dust.
Her secret garden.

Winning the Lottery

I.
Mom chooses me. I see the big picture.
        My demanding job, my busy husband.

She can't live here. She needs structure.
        A social life. Handrails.

I check facilities for safety, smells, services.
        Cost, convenience, comfort.

Heads or tails? Her new home,
        an independent living facility.

II.
She loves it. Makes many new friends.
        Widows, like her.

They play 56. She always wins.
        The star Bingo player, too.

Her visits with her best friend past midnight.
        Husbands, hobbies, kids.

"I have seven," Mom says.

        "I have two. One passed away."

"Oh, that's tragic. I'm so sorry. What about surgeries? I've had three, including a pacemaker."

    "I've had four!"

"That's so scary. My husband died. Two years gone."

    "Jim's gone too. I miss him. Ten years now."

"I take the blue meds. For the heart."

    "No, those pills are the pink ones."

They shake their heads. When the colors change,
    the memory snaps.

Trip to Gehenna
> *I used to walk behind you. Now you walk behind me.*
> *- Mom*

I.
A trip with Mom to see family. Just us girls.
        Buses and trains. Planes.

Can't recall. We haul two heavy bags
        from state to state.

Mom acts anxious, overly vigilant.
        Constantly checking her purse.

I can't leave her, but have to pee.
        The bathroom's across the station.

"Stay here, Mom." I hoof it to make a quick return.
        See her at a distance,

counting her cash. Flashing fistfuls of bills,
        Two hundred dollars, all in twenties.

A man's spotted her. His easy mark.
        I get to her first.

"Mom, put it away!"
        "Why should I?"

"People are watching! You'll get mugged!"

    I stare the jackal down. He retreats.

II.
It's time to go. The elevator, "Out of Service".
    Forced onto escalators

with two heavy bags on wheels! Mother, as steady as
    a ballerina balancing on a broken leg.

"Mom, be careful!" She runs ahead.

    "I'll be fine!"

Mom, excited and eager. Moving like a linebacker
    through the dense crowd.

The steep steps on the train.
    The porter's refusal to help Mom.

"Don't have liability."
    "You kidding me? If she falls, I can sue!"

Mom sits down. My seat's taken.
    Some schmoozing guy,

Who won't surrender his seat! Mom won't move.
    Not even for her daughter!

They're talking, laughing, like old friends.
        She's left me for another.

Our road trip. Just us girls. What folly!
        I feel left on the church steps.

Helpless, riled, exhausted third wheel.
        I keep close watch.

No rest yet on this vacation. Who's this woman?
        Mother's doppelgänger?

III.
At my brother's, our room's upstairs.
        For Pete's sake!

Mom may take the wrong turn
        on her way to the bathroom.

Tumble down the stairs.
        I can't sleep.

At the beach, I scan the sand.
        Where's Mother now?

Hopefully not swimming. The sun's burning.
        Like my soul.

IV.
Onto my sister's. Or another brother's.
    Can't recall.

Same old roads. Another filthy bus.
    Tiny, sticky bathroom.

Mom must go, but only room for one.
    How to help her safely?

Leave our stuff? Lose our seats?
    Maybe get robbed?

It's a bumpy highway ride. Maybe she falls -
    then what?

V.
No peace on this dream trip
    with my new mother.

Too many states, too many siblings,
    and very little sleep.

Trip to Gehenna. For my sacrifice.
    Oh, dear God.

Mom's Journal

Thoughts swirl in autumn breeze,
        fallen linden leaves.

    "Call Barbara."
        "Dentist, 10:00am."
    "Balance checkbook."
        "Bingo, tomorrow. 1:00pm."

    I gift her a journal to capture
fleeting reminders. Record her life stories.
    The thing about memory:
You have to remember
    that you have a journal.

    "Today is April 27, 2009.
I am trying to think of something
you may like to read. I am not
a good writer of anything.
My life has been good,
and at this point in time
I am eighty-two and living in an apartment building
for older people. I am mostly busy all day
playing cards, taking two-mile walks in the building,
playing bingo, selling things in our store
and everything I can find to do.
We can go to the stores by taking our bus
if we want. They also take us on trips

to other places or for groceries, church, etc.
It is a nice place to live.
My apartment is a one-bedroom. It
has a living room, small kitchen, and bathroom.
The building has other size apartments.
I miss seeing my family that is spread out.
I have seven children, and two of them live here
in town. I see them every Sunday.
They are in the same neighborhood,
so we spend the day together after church."

Bundling Blankets

I.
Another cold winter Sunday. I wait outside.
        Here she comes.

"Where's your coat?"

        "The sun's out."

"It's freezing today. You'll get sick."

        "No, I won't. The car's warm.
        I'll be fine."

II.
At my brother's. She isn't comfortable.
        "It's so cold!"

"Here's a sweater. And a soft comforter.
        Is that better?"

We play cards, compete, cuddle, do puzzles,
        watch old movies to help Mom's memory,

eat dinner. Argue, laugh, cry.
        Our typical family Sunday.

III.
"I'm sorry, Mom. Time to go.
        Put these on."

I offer my brother's warm coat. His woolen gloves.
        Sometimes a hat.

"Why should I?"

        "It's freezing outside."

"The sun's out!"

        "It's 9:00pm. With arctic winds."

"Where's *my* coat?"

        "At your place."

"Why's it *there*?"

I learn fast to stow coats,
        blankets and extra sweaters.
              for such days.

Mom's Pickles

I used to take care of you. Now, you take care of me.
-Mom

The answering machine
impatiently beeps
like an ambulance siren.

Message 1.
    The caller's voice drones.

    "Hon, I'm in a pickle."

        Sigh

    "My insurance dropped me."

        Sigh

    "The girl didn't come today. Again."

        Sigh

    "Call me."

        Click

Message 2.
    I hear a sigh.

    "Hello, Hon. I'm in a pickle."

    Sigh

    "My checkbook's missing."

    Sigh

    "And I'm diabetic. Just found out."

    Sigh

    "Call me."

    Click

Message 3.
    The voice catches.

    "Hello, Hon. It's Mom. I'm in a pickle."

    Sigh

    "There was a man in my room last night."

    Sigh

"At the foot of my bed."

Sigh

"Call me."

Click

Mom's Never Wrong

I.
"How are you?" Mom's new doctor's
 attentive to her.

Deaf to the daughter. Not *his* patient.
 She's suspect.

Must sign forms.
 Get proper permission.
  HIPAA HIPAA hurray!

 "I'm just fine." Mom scowls.
  Crosses her arms.

 Standing behind her, I shake my head.
  No! No! No!

 "Mom, your leg. It hurts, right?"
  I look at the doctor.

  "Not at all." Mom's suddenly stoic.

 "You fell remember? Outside of the mall."

  "I'm just fine."

I mouth "No!"
    The doctor listens. "Does this hurt?"

    "Ouch! Stop that!"

"What's the year?"

    "Who really cares."

"Who's the president?"

    "Don't know - Nixon?"

"What's your address?"

    "Check your files!"

"Is today Monday?"

    "Don't you know?"

My heart sinks. The same test results.
    As the last two tests showed.
        She has Alzheimer's.

II.
"What's wrong *here*?" He looks concerned.

Mom's feet stink with shedding dried skin.
        Layers of it.

I'm shocked, embarrassed.
        Missed the signs.

A Type 2 Diabetic. She's not doing
        the required foot care.

I taught her, but she forgot.
        I failed to do it for her. I failed.

III.
In the car, she again asks, "Where are we going?"

        "To the drugstore."

"Why?"

        "For some supplies."

"Why?"

        "For your feet." I explain again. Softly.

"They're just fine!" All of a sudden -
    Bam, Bam, Bam!

She clobbers me! In heavy traffic!
    I maneuver through the thwacks.

She won't recall, but I will.
    The very day we almost died.

I'm her guide.
    Even to God?

Held without Bond

I.
Mom's meds disappear far too soon.
She denies errors.

She's never wrong, but I am.
So is Walmart –

That's her claim.
She's no liar!

I hire aides for daily help,
imprison the pills in a strong box

with a secret combination,
and place it out of reach

on top of the fridge
behind the chips.

II.
Late night call.
       I feel dread.

"It's night security.
       There's a problem."

"Is she okay?"
        My stomach burns electric.

"It's her pills. They're locked up."
        I explain why.

"Oh, I see. That's too bad.
        Won't report this."

Won't report this?
        Is this prison?

Mother, the felon.
        With ice picks, knives.

Pounding, stabbing, jabbing.
        Can't break out.

Playing Cards Right

I find her in the library.
    The joyous partier,
        surrounded by friends,
laughing and regaling.
    Playing 56.
        Mom, the victor.

How she cackles.
    Rubs her victory in.
        Sweeps up pennies, nickels and dimes
to sort later into old checkbook boxes.
    She sits upright. Her chest out.
        Not a worry. My heart rises.

Then she spots me.
    Her body collapses.
        The wilting lily.
Devoid of spirit.
    Fraught with fragility.
        She requires care.

That barefaced transformation.
    It speaks volumes.
        She's two mothers.
Her telephone calls.
    "Hon, I'm in a pickle."
        For real, Mom?

Her sudden façade.
        To justify something?
                Meeting my expectations?
A miserable mother?
        That's not my desire!
                Who wants that!

I play dumb.
        "Mom, it's me!
                How's it going?"
I rub her back.
        Bravely greet her friends.
                The imposter wins.

Holding Out Soap

I'm stubborn, delusional.
        Perhaps even blind.
                Holding out hope
that Mother will recover.
        Return to me.
                My real Mom, the one

who loves shopping,
        having some lunch,
                getting her steps.
We're off to Panera.
        Then to Target
                where disaster strikes

in the bathroom.
        Explosive, smelly, vile.
                All over her,
her orthopedic shoes,
        and the tile floor,
                and her smoldering pride -

or is it my shame that reeks?
        People in line
                judging the daughter?
I feel naked. Exposed soiled soul.
        How selfish of me to fear derision
                as *Mom* is suffering!

"Mom, Gimme your purse.
        Stay here!"
                Will she remember?
I sprint to Penney's
        for new panties,
               socks, shoes, clothes.

I find a brave smile on sale
        for my return to Gehenna
              for another rescue.
Clean things up. Preserve our honor.
        Surrender to –
               just surrender.

Senior Alert

I.
High rent but no major expenses.
A clean environment. Convenience.

Two meals daily. Laundry facilities across the hall.
Parties, Bingo, outings.

But no more. She's changed.
May wander. Get lost. Face injury.

II.
I'm always torn. Mom or career?
Mom or marriage?

Mom or my own sanity?
The ungrateful daughter.

I make arrangements
for Mom's doctors' appointments.

The dreaded call,
      "Where's your mom?"

The aide arrives to transport Mom,
but Mom's gone missing.

Has taken off, we are told,
with the director,

who abandons Mom outside the doctor's building
on a busy avenue!

Mom, alone and confused.
Gripping her walker and purse.

For Pete's sake! I give instructions.
      "Please no rides. I have them covered."

They don't listen. Mom is convincing.
Thinks *I'm* forgetting!

III.
Fortunately, she survives. Finds her way
into the building,

up the elevator to the second floor,
down the hall to the doctor's office

all by herself. Begs the question –
Am I needed?

When I find her in the waiting room,
I'm rankled iron.

Mom looks unfazed.
    "What's up, Hon?"

She's found.
I'm lost.

Irish Spring

I.
We learn quickly. *It doesn't pay
to lie to Mom.* The twitch of a lip.
The tremor of the tongue.
The glance down to the left.
The hands folded at the chest.
        She knows.

        After all, she had dreams
to be a cop. An avid reader
of Agatha Christie, Ellery Queen.
A fan of Perry Mason and Colombo.

        She can smell beer on your breath
five feet away. Detect a light kiss goodbye
under the porch light.
        The scent of a man on a blouse.

        Those of us who tell tales
recall the rancid taste of Irish Spring soap.
That green stone-tough bar sitting
beside the kitchen sink.
        Handy.

She holds the head down.
With vigor, scrubs the toilet bowl clean.
The stubborn hard-water ring.
    The stench of deceit.

    The Truth Sayer, she declares our innocence.
A young mother accuses me of not changing her baby,
suffering from diarrhea. Mom knows
I won't leave a baby to blister red.
    Especially for that young widow
        finally out on a date.

    That integrity, bred into me
by Mom's Irish Spring temper.
Character, hard earned. Yet pliant.
Capable of slipping thorough the fingers
like a wet soap bar. I learn to keep my hands
    clean and dry.
        Or else.

II.
    I struggle with Mom's lapsing memory.
Her life dissolving before me. My sorrow,
an overflowing dishwasher, a treacherous
    walk on a sudsy floor.

      All the calls to Medicare, Social Security,
her insurance companies. Their requirement
to get her permission to speak to them,
      to do her business in her presence.

      I send copies of the POA. Doesn't matter.
Finally, I cave, resorting to my own landline
      for my lies.

I claim I'm Mom.
      (Well, Mom and I do share a name.)

      "Your voice sounds so young!"

"I'm often told that." My throat gargles suds.

III.
      I come to changing my character
in Mom's whodunits. I'm now her co-conspirator.
Her Dr. Watson. The clues do not add up for me,
      but she is the master detective.

      As Mom's memory fails,
she tells me about her trip to Australia.
      She's never visited there.

      I play along, "How was your trip?"

I commiserate with her when she claims
the aide never comes despite the sign-in sheet
　　　　　at the front desk.

　　　Certainly, I worry
that she will solve the mystery
　　　　of who secretly crosses
the Irish Spring soap
　　　　off her weekly shopping list.

The Caregiver's Craft

I'm only a human, Mom,
seeking perfection in my care for you.
Weaving the yarn, like you taught

and retaught. I keep forgetting
to practice. You say my head
is always in my books.

I anchor my hook
into a rhythm in each row,
putting the colors of your care in place.

Counting the stitches,
like the meter in a poem.
Casting off. Crocheting my lines.

Each stitch a thought, a memory, a discovery.
What am I crafting for you?
Comfort or chaos?

Will everything turn out?
I study the creation,
pleased. Some rows

proclaim symmetry,
coherence to form. I revel
in the virtuosity, clarity of hue

as though I have hooked
into radiance. But other rows
meander like a stream,

wandering around the bed rocks.
Threads in some rows, weeds,
tangled in the mud of past despair.

Memories to be forgotten.
Words that should have been
left unsaid. Plans gone awry.

Fitful dreams. Diminished hope.
As though gripping this hook
cripples my thinking. My loving.

Where am I heading, Mom?
Do I have it right yet?
Your care and wellbeing?

Being a doting daughter. Daunting.
I'm only a human
        unraveling our knots.

An Unsanctioned Outing

I.
Upon turning out the light
and fluffing the pillow,
I see a line of people

walk past my bed
one by one in a trance.
Mom enters the room with her walker,

stepping in tune to the steady march
of vacant faces. *Am I dreaming?*
        "Mom? Mom!"

"Where're you going?"
        "To the bus!!"
"What!!"

I jump out of bed.
Join the line.
She can't just leave

like *this*. She'll wander off.
She forgets that I help her.
I have instructions,

> "Don't let her on the bus.
> I don't care what she says.
> I always give her rides."

Still, here she is
catching the bus
without a care.

II.
The bus fills up. The driver is new.
Very courteous.
Looks to be from India.

Mom's a beacon.
As people surround her,
I scan the crowd.

Always her Secret Service agent.
A man starts to flirt with her.
> *What's this dude up to?*

I can't elbow my way in.
Her purse, in plain sight.
I glare at him.

> "Mom! Come with me!
> Let's sit by this window.
> The view is great."

Night diminishes into dusk.
Beautiful clouds appear
through the open windows

as the bus ascends up an
endless spiraling route
into the blue wisps.

Eventually the bus stops
at a tremendous overlook.
        "Elysium," the driver announces.

Some riders gather up their heavy baggage.
Disembark. I see greeters offering
smiles and hugs. "You made it!"

III.
The flirty guy signals Mom
to visit with him by the overlook.
        Now where is she going!?

I study his face, small stature,
skinny arms, dark skin. Gandhi?
Not Gandhi.

Some kind of holy man
dressed like a guru,
hunched in a white shroud.

Bearded. Not bearded.
Very familiar. The driver?
Not the driver. I don't know

the connection to India.
Someone holy, of the cloth.
Maybe Middle Eastern? *Jesus?*

The guru and Mom laugh,
settle into comradery,
teasing each other.

The man is clever with puns.
Mom, a young girl,
giggling and coy.

He looks over at me. Twinkles.
  "You know me."
    Yes, so familiar.

I see it in his hands! The Holy Bible!
  He's a Reverend!
    "Dad!?"

IV.
The driver announces the bus's departure.
"All Aboard, Gehenna!" I motion for Mom
to follow me back to the bus.

Mom wants to stay with Dad.
I won't have it. Not yet. I'm not ready
We argue. She huffs,

stomps onto the bus
      "The next time I come here,
           I'm not leaving!"

V.
The following day,
I'm at Mom's residence
to pick her up for lunch

and give the director
a piece of my mind
for allowing her on the bus.

A new driver emerges
from the bus made ready
for the day's tour. A man from India.
      The very same man who steered that bus
          into God's crystalline eyes.

Mom's Purse

Has a comb, and a slot
for a dummy checkbook,

her real checkbook,
long ago gingerly removed

with her permission –
but she's forgotten.

Tissues and cough drops,
a small coin purse,

filled with pennies,
nickels and dimes for 56

and Bingo. A wallet
with some cash,

but no more twenties
to fan to the loitering boys.

Her driver's license,
out of service.

Her Social Security card,
having slipped away

into my care
as have her doctors' numbers,

their specialties, her med list,
appointments, insurance cards.

Through a tear in the lining,
her memories linger as lint.

Bookends

Not enough that I am
the spitting image of Mom
and her namesake.

We both experienced
a brain injury. The encephalitis
burned away my young memories;

      Alzheimer's, her short-term ones.

Before falling ill, I recalled
story books word for word.
Afterwards, I needed constant

review to memorize a story line.
Master a school lesson.
Learn names.

      Mom isn't able to watch a movie
      without confusion or follow the storyline
      in the novels I read aloud.

The main thrill - hearing the name
of her hometown
in Steve Hamilton mysteries.

After encephalitis, I fell mute. Words,
always sitting on the edge of my tongue
or invented. "Infelicitous", said the professor.

    The same for Mom.
    Her thingamajigs
    and whatchamacallits
    keep me guessing.

Encephalitis put me in a wheelchair.
    Mom has ended up in one.

I taught myself how to walk again.
    Mom has weakened.

Encephalitis made me sensitive
to bright lights, loud sounds, crowds.

    Alzheimer's makes it difficult for Mom
    to endure commotion.

I still have problems
with focus and fatigue,
    and so does she,
    especially at twilight after
    a busy day.

After encephalitis,
I saw angels and ghosts.

    Mom asks, "Who's that man?"

"Which man, Mom?"

    "The one who just walked in.
    Standing right behind you."

So I understand her shelf of sorrow,
how it bows with the weight of it all.

But just as she held up my end,
    I hold up hers.

Grandmother Lilian

I.
I love the name Lily,
that consoling grief
holding up its stem
leaning forward
to brush the bereaved
passing by.

II.
You were a tender lily, Grandmother,
avoiding crowds, cameras,
any display of your grace.
You retreated to tend to your garden
and the house. I hardly got to know you.
We lost you when I was just five.

My only memory, what Mom told me,
how she felt unmothered.
At the age of three, she rode her tricycle
down to the Soo locks,
where sailors waved
at a lonely girl.

Your other girls, Grandmother.
One died from influenza in 1919.
The other from crib death in 1934.
Did you feel it was your fault,
being the wife of a well-respected surgeon,
whose babies died in your care?

You didn't tell your husband
about the stabbing pains
in your broken heart
that took you too young.

III.
Mom, the sorrow was shared.
It was not so much
your longing for your mother -
it was *her* longing for you.
Her love for you

was too fragile to share.

The loss of your sisters
built a wall around her soul
to shield the crumbling petals of grief.
Losing yet another daughter

would be unbearable.
You were left with the ghosts -
the specters of what could have been -
had your mother - and sisters –
not abandoned you.

Mom and I Play Lassos with Our Hysterectomy Scars

I.
Mom's scar can stretch from any corner of the country
       to Mid-Missouri.

A thick rope of Mother Wound
       reaching for my root.

Her scar deepens as age swells her skin,
draping the wound on her lap.

       I am tethered to her lesion. The grief
       rubs my neck raw.

Out of her wound spills her love.
Her lava shapes my landscape, devours me.

       Creates loss as all that I can mother
       is burned away.

While Mom earns her scar,
       mine is prescribed by Diethylstilbestrol.

The motherless are called orphans.
       What are the childless called?

I bear my hysterectomy scar for what?
       To spare my unborn my trauma?

II.
The unmothered can mother
>	the one who will be childless.

Bearing children fills the chasm
of her mother's inattention.

>	My broken womb is the crypt holding the soul
>	of my unborn daughter.

Mom has seven, so she wins the Gold.
>	I have hopes but don't qualify.

Our scars are vaults.
>	Hers for the renown.
>>	Mine for the unnamed.

Her scar nurtures a bountiful garden.
>	Mine stocks a stillroom of recalled goods.

III.
One who is childless
>	can still mother the unmothered.

Her scar says to me, "Don't forget me."
>	Mine says to her, "Stay close."

Hers forms a cane.
    Mine ties bundles of blankets
        to keep her warm.

Hers is the IV torn from her wrist
    at her end of days.

    Mine is the string of pearls that matches
        her last Easter dress.

Mud Maid

Mother, dressed in
moss and lichens,
a perch for owls.
Her hair, luscious grass.
She rests on a path at Heligan
for a long nap in the sun
of lost gardens
and timeless nights.
Though it is written,

"Don't come here
to sleep or slumber".

3

ECHO

"What have you done to me, Barbara Ann?"

I Betray Her
> *It's Hell growing old.*
> *-Mom*

Mom's friends die, one by one.
> She's lonely, lost.

I'm distraught, disheartened. She's failing,
> needs assisted living.

We always talk. Decide things together,
> though she forgets.

We face the dreaded conversation,
> do the math.

Full-time aides. Plus her rent.
> Eight thousand monthly. Impossible.

Her happy times
> now crushed autumn leaves.

I concede defeat,
> face the winter storm.

The hooting owls flee with her grief
> and my sorrow.

Once she's moved, she glares daggers.
    "What have you
        done to me?!"

House of Sand

I.
      A new welcoming residence. They give her furniture. Show her around.

      Assign her a seat in a pleasant dining area.
Lots of activities, like Bingo and movies.

      Full-time nursing. Her meds secure. I feel hopeful, grateful for respite.

      I'm kidding myself! The next day,
Dreaded news.

"Your mother fell."

      Classes get covered. I gather Mom and her walker
for a day at Urgent Care and the ER.

      The hours pass sluggishly. I observe other daughters with their elderly parents.

      What would these people do
without their children?

      What will I do?
I have no children.

II.
  The usual case. Mom is unharmed,
but we're exhausted.

  Finally, we're back at the new place.
Nurses and social workers arrive

   to make her acquaintance. Too much commotion
fills her room.

  Mom needs rest
and definitely clean clothes.

  "Please help her?" I ask politely, handing nurses clothing.

I hear a scuffle in the bathroom. Mom groans in pain.

  "What's going on?"

  One nurse snaps, "She's being combative!"

My tsunami rises. Words slap rapidly.

  "You will not.
  Talk to her.
  Or about her.
  In that tone!"

This place sucks. I lose confidence,
    complain to management.

III.
    Still more problems with the same contrary nurse.

"If she falls. We can't help. She's too heavy."

Back to management. What's assisted living!?
I don't mince words.

"Do her right. That's your job! - Or she moves!"

Whenever I arrive. They fall silent.
    Waiting for my tsunami.
        Fine with me.

Mom and Elvis

Mom's place prepares. Tables are set.
Lights turned low.

The King arrives. With his band
and backup singer.

Elvis still lives. Fifties' hair waves.
Thick side burns.

Svelte sexy style. Tight sleek pants.
Shiny collared shirt.

Opened just so. A V-chest reveal.
Blue suede shoes.

Deep brown eyes. Like his voice.
A tinge sad.

He ain't nothin'. Just a hound.
Looking for trouble.

Mom's smiling coyly. Falling in love.
Good for her.

I'm no fan. Not this one.
Death mimics life.

This guy's flirtatious. Just like Elvis.
Making the rounds.

Women are clapping. Pick me! Me!
Waving their hands.

He's behind me. My skin's crawling.
He leans over.

Cameras are snapping. Go to Mom.
Please, go away.

He reads minds. Moves to Mom.
She's lovin' it.

Brought to life. By the dead.
All shook up.

Fool's Gold

Assisted living, a mythology.
Mom's not bathing
or changing clothes.

Probably not sleeping. Just sits up,
waiting for breakfast.
They don't force her to comply

after three tries. Company policy.
Like limited staffing. After dinner hours.
And on weekends.

I can join Mom during meal times. Mom waits,
holding her coffee cup. Her table mates,
sharp and chatty.

Mom, flat and detached.
My fear. That she's gone.
Now for good.

Just one friend, Mary, across the hall.
Mom needs me. No one else.
I'm her ponderous love.

Mom's shifting demeanor.
Like a trickster.
She's two mothers.
        One for me.
                One for Elvis.

The Marauding Jackals

Still her advocate. Checking for incompetency.
        Surveilling, challenging, assessing.
I always notice the unmade bed, the dirty blouse.
        Greasy hair. What's going on?
It's worse now.

She refuses again and again. Especially if I'm visiting.
        Then what happens?
Nurses have tea? Surf the web?
        The missing Depends, openly taken for others.
Are they replaced?

"Where's your ring?"

        "She took it."

"Who took it?"

        "The girl did. To admire it. Then she left."

I look everywhere. Count her valuables.
        Feel helpless. Angry.
It's Mom's word against the other woman's.
        Whoever she is.
Mom has Alzheimer's. Who's going to win
        this debate?

It's just a ring. But Grandma Hattie's ring.
    Meant for me!
I remove valuables, quickly and quietly.
    Replace them with imitations.
Look at me, the deceiver. I face reprimand
    and an Irish Spring bath.

My aching heart for the orphaned elderly,
    confused prey for jackals
nabbing the gems and crying, "LIAR!"
    Will they scrounge
for other jewels? Clean her out?
    Thieve her soul?

I must keep watch. The morning hawk.
    The moonlit owl.

Angels Give a Hoot

I.
She lingers on my right side.
Why the right? An owl hoots
by the window for three nights.

Pennies appear out of nowhere
when I've earned
an angel wing.

I dread her birthday,
the first since she left.
No more cake, cards, gifts.

II.
I relive her end of days. That call.
"Your mother isn't well."
The ER. The hours waiting. Suddenly

the examination room fills quickly.
Tachycardia. She's admitted.
Heart and kidney failure.

Nothing can be done.
I call family. How
can this be happening?

I'm curled in a window well, sobbing.
Onlookers pass by slowly,
viewing my body.

I stay with her each night
to guard the IVs
until we move her

to a place with terminal care,
where a bedraggled nurse says,
"No one may stay with her overnight."

We gradually break that rule as
her body fights her. A child is always
at her bedside. To keep watch.

III.
Her children rally for her.
Hold her close. Feed her.
Comb her hair. The reunion

she's always wanted.
She holds on for days,
greedy for our love.

IV.
Gregoria's chants
take her in and out of her room.
She speaks the language

of angels. Not English.
How they argue.
Divine negotiation

with pacing, intonation,
logical pauses, stressed
and unstressed syllables.

Meant for me - a linguist - to hear.
Her voice, husky, deep. Ancient.
Is this how it goes?

Contracts? Debts due?
Life purpose fulfilled?
Is there free will?

> "No. Not now.
> I need to pack.
> Pay some bills."

> "No. Not ready.
> I have this reunion.
> Everyone's here".

> "No. I beg you.
> I've been reckless.
> God will judge."

V.
Ultimately terror grips her
as she faces
the indescribable,

pushing it away
with such force,
we fear *this is it*.

Debate and battle
give way to stillness
and surrender.

Departing from Gate 3

I.
How will she manage
the mysterious passage?
This woman with no memories,

no way to find the path,
recall a friend, her mother,
recognize the welcoming

Angel of Death?
Will she need me
to take her hand?

We hold her close,
      "Go to the light. Look for Dad."
But will she?

      "Light? Dad?"
Her last breaths soft breeze,
Does she know it's the end?

The chakras still spin
until spent into ashes.
No wind. No turmoil.

My heart collapses.
Her guide and now
not her guide.

Her daughter
and now
her orphan.

II.
In a dream, there she is,
resting peacefully
on a plush bed in an alcove.

Curtains draped
on either side. Her shoes,
placed gingerly under the bed.

"I'm in a pickle! Where's my wallet?"

I find her purse and checkbook.
Pay the last bill.

III.
Three shiny pennies
line up perfectly in a row
on hot asphalt.

"Pick them up."
I refuse.
 Resist her omen –

> "My passage commences
> on April third. The tickets.
> Nonrefundable."

Mermother: A Rogue Dream Poem
-After Melanie Figg

I.
Mother sits, her back to me.
How can I see into her eyes,
into her maelstrom of memories,

tossing and turning thoughts,
clouds reflected in vertiginous waves.
Watching for mishaps,

I guide her onto a life boat.
"Where do you want me, Hon? Here?"
       "Sit there, please."

She sits elsewhere.
I salvage the bills and pills,
her CPAP for clear and calm dreams.

"Whatever you want, Hon."
       "Not what I want. What you need."
She removes the mask when I leave.

II.
She slips away into tumbling waves.
Mermother, her stories of elusive coral treasure.
Her travails with Kulilu and Melusina. Rescues

of sailors who solved her riddles. Her songs
with her lover, Trewhella. Her battle with Hecate
to retrieve her pearls.

Suddenly I am her octopus friend.
I gather her in my arms
and swim up for air.

III.
The good days at the mall,
shopping for rings, new handbags,
Alfred Dunner outfits.

Lunch at Panera's, ice cream
at Café Court and a movie. At Hallmark,
we shop for sympathy cards.

I am spending too much money.
        My husband says, "You have to.
                She's your mother."

IV.
When the storm waves recede,
I find my mermother laid to rest on the shore,
her string of pearls broken.

Her eyes meet mine. I wipe her gills.
Her lips turn blue
and pulse to stillness.

Mom's Dreams

You wanted to be a police officer.
How did the curriculum at Lindenwood College
fit that dream? I never asked to see
the course listings. You dropped out
during your freshman year.
I didn't want to pry.

You couldn't attain that goal.
A mother of 7. Your full-time job.
Your legs swelled from hours
cooking meals from scratch and baking bread.
Canning whatever the parishioners donated.
Corn, beans, tomatoes. Your delicious pickles!

You crocheted, knitted, and sewed,
creating the huge piles
under the Christmas tree.
Still, you had free time for us.
The walks to town to shop. Hamburgers and fries
at Pete's Café on Main Street. The afternoon matinées.

The way you interacted with people in public.
I imagined the friendly neighborhood cop,
back in the day, visiting with people on his beat.
Consoling them. Offering advice. Sharing,
not shooting. You drew people to your light.
The reason why you were a popular pastor's wife.

For someone who felt unmothered,
you knew the mother's code of ethics and love.
We were your world and your work.
What we learned from you we took with us.
I minored in sociology and volunteered
for the Rape Crisis Center.

Taught a Family-to-Family course
for the National Alliance on Mental Illness.
Volunteered for the hospice that helped you.
Your oldest son, a policeman, public
servant and a volunteer for the Shriners.
One sister devoted her career as a social worker

to serve the LGBTQ community.
My other sister, influenced by you and Dad,
became a minister and hospice chaplain.
I see your genius and gumption
in my young brothers, who excelled in life
without college degrees. Highly successful

self-taught computer program creators,
computer technicians, and prepress artists.
In each child I see the greatest of your gifts.
To show compassion for others.
You always taught us to be kind.
When others hurt us, they are suffering.

Were we ever unmothered?
I see now how depleted you were at times.
Lost in your mystery novels and romances.
Once we left home, you hung up your crochet
hooks.

Put your heart in the freezer to thaw
on special occasions. Greeted our visits
with a silence that made us feel
that love is labor. Love is loss.

Mom, rest assured. Your oversight
and affection taught us
how to weave our worlds
gilded with your love.

The Phone of the Wind
-In homage to Itaru Sasaki

  Whispers to you, my lost mother,
on the phone of the wind.
The storm of Alzheimer's
has washed away your well-constructed
mind, your recipes, your photo albums.
  Our plans.

  Our connection now,
a rotary phone
inside Itaru's booth
sitting atop a hill
overlooking a valley.
No dial tone. Just the murmurs
  of the caller's breath.

  Itaru built this phone booth
to contact his young cousin, taken by cancer.
Speaking to the wind,
  making rain of his tears,
    calms his sorrow.

  He offers us this chance.
Can it be this simple?
  This profound?

I haven't forgotten your number, Mom.
Each finger traces the circular path,
releases and sighs. I wait for you
    to pick up.

I strain to catch your voice
in my throat. I bear my burdens
    into the wind.

You were always the wisest. Gradually,
I had to have all the answers for your care.
I couldn't hold onto you. The rising waters
washed you away. You, the mother I knew.
Oblivious to your own
    drowning.

After the wind swept your mind away,
I thought you left me a message on my cell. I struggled
to hear your excited words.
Your static slowly dissipated
    like fog lifting to reveal a new meadow.

My siblings and I crowd around
the phone booth of the wind,
taking turns to share our news,
to seek advice, to say
    goodbye.

You taught us well. We survive
our own catastrophes. Broken dreams.
    Broken health.
        Broken hearts.

Good news, too! New grandchildren.
Milestones. Awards. Honors.
    We still seek your praise.

    Relief that you've missed the pandemic.
The collapse of civility. The political
    eruptions. Mass shootings. Earthquakes.
        Polar floods.
            Exile to Mars.

    The phone trills as we dial.
We hear our whispers
    echo your name.

Marie Kondo Cleans My Purse at Starbucks

Konmari sees me at Starbucks.
My purse spills over on the counter.
"May I help?"

She gathers me up
like I'm antique lace
washed too many times.

Before she begins, she whispers,
"Hello, the House,
I am safe. May I enter?"

She pokes through my purse,
pulling out the deck of cards
Mom once carried in her own purse.

A heavy bag of Mom's pennies
to redeem for cash.
Her checkbook.

The messy calendar
that listed her appointments
alongside my own.

The quilt she made me,
now falling apart. A cookbook
compiled in her own hand.

Konmari extracts other artifacts,
laying them gently on lined up tables.
People gather. My eyes bleed.

The extra-large pair of panties
Mom made me wear to Sunday school.
The wash, still not done.

A half-used bottle of Diethylstilbestrol
she was prescribed to prevent spotting
when I was in utero.

The tricycle she rode
around town at age three
because her mother never watched her.

My cancer scares, scattered
on the bottom of the purse
like cookie crumbs.

The scabs inflicted
by her compression stockings
I failed to wash one last time.

The clump of tissue
I miscarried, swaddled
in an inner pocket.

Her hysterectomy scar.
My hysterectomy scar.
Entwined on a spool.

My t-shaped uterus,
clenching a half-used packet
of Puffs Plus.

A dogeared photo of Mom.
A mirror reflecting
who I want to be.

Konmari has me
hold each item
one last time, saying,

"Thank you, tiny soul,
for sharing your life. I am
grateful."

She teaches me
how to fold joy
three times.

How to throw out
what I can
no longer carry.

Mom's Promise

I wonder what will happen
if you forget me, Mom.
I think you will say,

"You're so much nicer
than my daughter Barbara!"

You say, "If I forget
who you are, please remember
I love you.

I would never mean
to hurt you!"

Farewell, My Flower

How short
was your stay!
I took you for granted. Promised
I would stop by
more often.

I was too caught up
in my mindless days
to sit with you in your garden.
Your lush blooms
made the sun smile.

Your poise.
Your grace. Holy gifts.
Even when the snow
surprised us all,
you held your back up.

Your crown, never drooping.
Your resilience
tricked me
into complacency.
Still, you danced.

Until your beauty
crumbled
into the beds of periwinkle
huddled
to catch you.

Until the breeze
gently blew
your ash
into soil.

"Thinking of You"
-a card from Mom

This sentiment on the front fold -
Is this a sympathy card
or a show of support?

I'm looking through files
for letters from Mom,
nothing turns up.

Dad, the writer.
Mom adds notes.
    "Thoughts as warm"

as "Your father's condition
should be taken seriously",
written in cursive with large loopy eyes.

I picture her taking the cap off the pen,
scripting a note with precision,
recapping the pen,

unlike me, who failed
in "Completes Work Neatly",
my scrawls, as bold

    "as sunlight"
etching letters into burned trails
on the page.

Tidying up, I find this card,
sandwiched between napkins
and mail ready to toss.

   "Thinking of You"
crafted like Mom wrote it.
The front fold,

the color of Mom's birthstone,
displays lilacs
   "spilling through a window"

The inside fold, warm greetings
   "are with you today."
    Love, Mom

Then she pens,

"I hope your birthday's bright,
and you have many more.
I'm so happy you came into my life.
I can't think how much I love you
or admire you."
   Love, Mom (again)

This choral echo,
    "Love, Mom."
        "Love, Mom."

A hymn's reverberation?
    "Ah - men."
        "Ah - men."

It could resound a reminder,
    "Love Mom."
        "Love Mom."

Any mother's enduring
hopes or dreams
for her daughter's love.

Or possibly Hyperion's provoking inquiry,
    "Love your Mom?"
        "Love your Mom?"

And my reply,
    "Why, yes, Hyperion!"
        "Yes, I do!"
            "I surely do!"

Acknowledgments

I am very grateful for all the loving encouragement and feedback from my family, especially my husband, Dierik, who was very supportive of my development as a poet and my time commitment to this collection; and my sister Martha Harris, who proofread early drafts of this poetic memoir.

My gratitude also goes out to my siblings and extended family, who understood my journey with Mom and never doubted my care for her. My brother Monty Harris and his wife, Linda, were also devoted caregivers to Mom. I am grateful to many poets and writers for their support for this ongoing memoir and peer edits of some of the poems: Walter Bargen, Matt Dube, Sharon Feltman, Lynne Jensen Lampe, Cortney Daniels, Lois Long, Zak Wardell, Cam Whelr, Blair Kilpatrick, Judith Walton Comer, Winifred Morice and Ken Gierke.

I would like to extend extra warm gratitude to Matt Dube and Sharon Feltman for reviewing and editing an early draft and to Lynne Jensen Lampe for sharing in our first-book publication journeys.

I deeply appreciate the critical acclaim provided by Missouri's first Poet Laureate, Walter Bargen, and editors Kristiana Reed, James Diaz, and Jill McCabe Johnson.

This collection came together while I was taking Alison Wearing's course, Memoir Writing, Ink. I have found Wearing to be very supportive of my journey as a memoirist. Without her instruction, I may not have identified the memoir's "container" (three pennies), story arc, triggers, and overarching theme for this poetic memoir.

I would like to thank The Alzheimer's Association for their advocacy and research into this devastating disease. https://www.alz.org

For information about Diethylstilbestrol (DES): https://www.cancer.gov/about-cancer/causes-prevention/risk/hormones/des-fact-sheet

For information about Encephalitis: The Encephalitis Society. https://www.encephalitis.info/

Credits

Versions of these poems are found in the following places.
Anti-Heroin Chic (October 2021): "Mother's Light".

extraordinarysunshineweaver.blog (2017- 2020): "Mud Maid", "Picking Blueberries with Mom", "Farewell, My Flower."

Free Verse Revolution: A literary magazine (2021-2022), "Hestia for Hire", "Mermother: A Rogue Dream Poem", "My Mother's Vanity".

Phoebe MD: Medicine & Poetry (2020): "Erosion"; "This Brittle Seed" (as "Hope Was Not A Loss")

Spillwords, "Cooking a Life with a Wire Spine" as a featured post and nominated for Publication of the Month (August 2021). "Marie Kondo Cleans My Purse at Starbucks" won Publication of the Month for January/February (2022).

Well Versed 2020: "Woman".

Wombwell Rainbow (2022), "Erosion"

In *Wounds I Healed: The Poetry of Strong Women* (Experiments in Fiction 2022), "Mom's DES Baby: The Hardest Pill to Swallow" and "Ode to the Embryo that My T-Shaped Uterus Miscarried"

Notes

The epigraph on the dedication page, "Where thou art - that - is home", is from Emily Dickinson's poem #725.

In the poem "Mom and Elvis", some phrases recall Elvis tunes: "Ain't Nothin' But a Hound Dog", "All Shook Up", "Blue Suede Shoes".

www.ingramcontent.com/pod-product-compliance
Lightning Source LLC
Chambersburg PA
CBHW072055110526
44590CB00018B/3184